#SELFIE

Take One: Behind Every Smile Is An Untold Story

CARITA MONTGOMERY

#SELFIE

Copyright © 2016 Carita Montgomery

All rights reserved. No part of this book may be reproduced or transmitted in any form or by any means without written permission of the author.

ISBN: 978-0-9837182-7-7

Library of Congress Control Number: 2016941657

Perfectly Imperfect Publishing Company, LLC

Printed in the United States of America

Acknowledgements

Thank you to my Lord and Savior Jesus Christ for blessing me with uncommon wisdom. I am so grateful for every opportunity you have bestowed upon me.

To my husband, Leon, who has been so supportive and loving throughout this entire journey. To my children, I love you dearly. To my mother, Betty Johnson, for always encouraging and inspiring me.

Now to the three beautiful women who contributed their stories to this project. You all have a special place in my heart. Petrea Lovejoy, thank you for your unwavering support and advice throughout this venture. Natarsha Garcia, who served as my mentor, thank you for everything. You birthed something great in me. Last but not least, Natasha Cozart for our special "pep talks" during the editing process. I love you all!

A heartfelt thanks to my publisher and editor-in-chief, Lakia Brandenburg. Much gratitude to Christie Blackwell, the transcriber for the manuscript. A special thanks to the design team for the cover and to my photographers, Divine and B. Alyssa.

Let's Take a #SELFIE

As the author of #SELFIE, my ultimate goal is to uplift, inspire, and motivate you. I want to see you win in every area of your life. I want to see you shake off the disappointments and rise again. I am publishing this book for the sole purpose of helping others to see that when life throws you lemons, you better take them and make lemonade, lemon meringue pie, Lemonheads—okay, you get the point. Lemons suggest sourness or difficulty in life, while lemonade is a sweet drink. I want you to have optimism and a positive *can do* attitude in the face of adversity or misfortune.

#SELFIE is writing down what's on our minds which is a great way to work through inner conflict and process your feelings around a particular situation. It strengthens you when you take inventory of your life in written form. When God laid it on my heart to proceed with the #SELFIE book project, he also showed me the sea of women who would be inspired and motivated by its contents. The vision was then given with more clarity. Not only would I take my own written #SELFIE, but I would invite three other powerful women—my contributors—to do the same.

With the perfect lighting and the right angle, your front camera can capture a perfect image of your face. With a pen and courage, you can capture the perfect image of your life that will inspire so many around you.

What you are about to read is full of transparency, genuineness, and honesty—all for the purpose of providing you with encouragement, hope, forward-thinking and above all, the drive to never give up. Come take this journey with us as we flip the pen and take a #SELFIE.

Just as I brought these incredible women along with me, I want you to do the same. Share #SELFIE with your friends, family, co-workers, and associates. Let's start a global awareness of taking a #SELFIE with a pen and how it changes your entire outlook on life. Have fun with it. Be free with it. And break down the walls and live. I can already see the hundreds of thousands of #SELFIEs.

Remember, you are never in it alone. We are here rooting for you, sending positive energy your way. We are empowering you to take action today. I feel the movement happening all around us. We have the power to promote change to anything we set our minds to. I just love what I see happening for each of you who take your very own #SELFIE.

Contents

Carita Montgomery – A Decision to Choose 1

Petrea Lovejoy – No Love Lost. .15

Natarsha Garcia – God Has a Plan. 31

Natasha Cozart – Six Feet Deep. 49

A Decision to Choose

We all make decisions. They have good and bad consequences. This chapter is about some of the decisions I have made in my life. I have come to the conclusion that nothing is wasted. No experience, no relationship, no tragedy is a waste. It's all working for our good and our growth. When there is something great on the inside of you, even those bad decisions can't hold you away from what is destined for you—even in the lowest of these moments when I questioned everything about my existence, and when I questioned God for allowing these things to happen to me. The low times literally robbed me of years—ten years of my life. I was depressed and didn't know it. I ate and slept away my thirties. I became tainted, judgmental, mean, and irritable. I believed in God, but I did not know how to trust him.

As I open up and share my life with you, I pray that you will see the greatness that's on the inside of you. I want you to know that you are not in this alone. As women, we endure so much. I was buried, living in a virtual grave for more than ten years—paralyzed in a sense. I felt like this dark storm cloud just hovered over me. There were moments when the sun shined, but the storm clouds overpowered them. I wanted to throw in the towel, run, cave in and quit. But one day I stopped believing all the lies that the devil was feeding me. I stopped running and hiding. I stopped letting the fear of what others thought of me consume me. I stopped apologizing for who I was. I stopped making excuses about my purpose and my greatness. I stopped pretending that everything was okay when I was dying on the inside.

Once I embraced my truth, I began to heal. Sharing my mistakes, trials, shortcomings, and other imperfections was in a way my therapy. I cried a lot, but that was my way of coping. I took back my life. There was always greatness on the inside of me. God has always had his hands on me. Even as a child, I saw myself in great places. I began to see myself differently. I began to see myself happy. I began to see myself successful. Literally, I started embracing who I was. I made a decision to love and be loved. I see you doing the same. I see you making a decision to choose life.

Decision to Choose Life

I met my husband, Leon, my senior year of high school and we immediately had a connection. He had a bit of a "bad boy" swag that I wasn't really sure about. But he would write me these beautiful letters and poetry and there was something very attractive about his ability to express himself on paper. His persistence finally paid off and we started dating in 1989. He was my high school sweetheart. To further our education, I chose Florida A&M University (FAMU) and he chose Morris Brown College. We were in a long distance relationship, but even though we were miles apart, we remained faithful to each other. In my sophomore year, I found myself in a situation where I was pregnant. I had to tell my family and they were very upset with me (rightfully so). They didn't believe that I should have the baby. They actually made the decision for me. I wasn't going to have the baby.

After I called my mom, within a week I had a bus ticket and a doctor's appointment set up. I told Leon what they had decided for me and he begged me not to do it. However, at the time, my family's decision outweighed his influence on my decision. Within twenty-four hours, I went to the appointment. The abortion was done and all of it was swept under the rug. We never talked about it again. But when I found myself in the same situation two years later, I felt tormented by it.

It was 1992 and I was in the Planned Parenthood office. My mind was spinning and racing with questions and doubts. *Why am I here? Why was I not more careful? I can't do this! I'm mad because I know better.* Tears were rolling down my face as I completed a stack of stupid forms! *When was your last period?* Seven weeks ago, I wrote.

I thought, *I can't use my real name. No one can know.* This was so embarrassing. I wanted to scream and just burst into an ugly cry! I had been dreading this for weeks. I made up a name: Lavette Jones. I was only nineteen years old and wasn't ready for this.

Have you ever been there? When your mind is just racing with negative thoughts and you suddenly feel like you are in a bubble in the world or in a room alone. I just looked up and begged God with everything in me. "Please God, help me! God make this all go away!" In that moment, I thought this was the end of the world. I knew how my family would view me. I couldn't call home with this again. I prayed to God. "Lord, please give me a negative pregnancy test. Please God, please!" Thoughts continued to flood my mind. *It's probably just stress. It couldn't possibly be a baby. I'm trying to finish college. What about my family? They will be disgusted with me, their pride and joy, "Ms. FAMU", the business major.*

Because I knew that my family would be equally as angry, I decided that I would tell them my news, but shut them out until it was well past the time period for a legal abortion. This time I decided I wasn't going to let them sway my decision and I was going to have the baby. Even though my decision was made, I still had all of these fears, doubts, and questions. I had gone against all of their philosophies, their beliefs, their religion—I went against it all. My grandfather was a deacon in the church and my family members were pillars of the church. I had their reputation to uphold. Up until that point, I had been the child with the clean track record. *Well, you might as well become a welfare queen,* I thought. I didn't want to get on public assistance. That was just humiliating. I looked up and begged God again as more tormenting thoughts entered my mind ... *I heard that daycare was so expensive.*

I could barely take care of myself. I even tried negotiating with God. "Lord, if you let this test be negative, I promise to turn my life over to you. I'll surrender all, I promise, Lord." The lady with the clipboard called out the name. It took me a minute to respond to the nurse, forgetting I had made it up. I stood up and followed the nurse to the back.

While pregnant, I wasn't allowed to attend church services. My family was so angry with me and they didn't want to be embarrassed and feel ashamed. I felt like an outcast. I saw how everyone else who had chosen to have their baby seemed to carry this negative cloud or have a less than ideal outcome. From my experience, you either ended up on welfare or with a deadbeat dad.

I remember how people would speak the worse about people in that situation. Now that I'm a parent of three, I understand why. I understand the punch-in-the-gut feeling when your child makes a mistake that the world can see. But now the hard part. I had to raise a child. This didn't kill me, but it made me stronger. For me, this was still *my* choice. And I was going to see it through.

Decision to Choose Marriage

My opinion is that marriage is good. I decided on August 8, 1998, to enter into sacred matrimony. To me, marriage is a covenant. It is a covenant between me and God. I don't think we can enter into or exit out of it lightly. I must uphold those words "…'til death do us part."

It is my decision to make this marriage work at all costs. As a wife, I believe my responsibility is to love, nurture, and guide my family. It is up to me to help instill spiritual values in the home and to support and submit myself under my husband as head of the household. But it didn't always work that way.

There have been times in my marriage when I felt like I was justified to leave, but something on the inside reminds me that this isn't just a lightweight agreement. This is a lifetime arrangement, not a business contract. I decided to stay in the marriage no matter what the struggles may be. But how much did I have to endure? There were many years of struggle. There were moments when I just wanted to jump into my car and run.

It's amazing how life just sucks up your fairytale, swallows it, and spits it back out in your face. The first fifteen years of my marriage were spent identifying the roles of husband and wife and learning how to raise our children. I was misguided in thinking that a submissive wife was a weak wife, so every argument or disagreement in our marriage was an all-out war. I felt like I had the right to be, to do, and to say whatever I felt. And so did my husband. There was no area of compromise or understanding for the other person's feelings or position. I did not know or have an example of what a successful marriage looked like between a husband and wife, nor did my husband. We were figuring it out as we went along and every choice wasn't necessarily the best one.

On New Year's Eve in 1998, I had been married for four and a half months. My husband and I had disagreed on how to celebrate the holiday. He went out and I chose to be filled with anger and malice. I took all of his clothes out the closet and threw them in a pile in the living room. He came home furious, and we got into a physical altercation. My child was five years old at the time. I was so embarrassed, but again my mission is that my story will bring about healing for someone. Police were called and we were both arrested. I lived the most horrific New Year's of my life. I cried and cried, and cried and cried. They took my fingerprints and mugshot, and we were incarcerated for two days before the hearing. This was just one of the many incidents in our marriage. It was either in uproar or a battle. Once again, by me not understanding my role and he not understanding his role, we were still trying to figure out how marriage worked.

We both decided that we didn't want to end the marriage. We wanted to work on the marriage and our life together. We went to counseling several times, but this time we decided to get spiritual counseling—which is one of the best things we had ever done. For the first time in our lives, we began to see our marriage from the Word of God and not from what our thoughts or experiences were. But we only continued the counseling for three weeks before we decided that it worked. We didn't want to do it anymore.

There were a lot of outside influences. I even found that friends would give bad advice and be unsupportive with nothing grounded in the Word of God. I had to decide that I wanted to fight for my marriage no matter what. It had come to a point where counseling was an issue because we could not agree on whether to go clinical or spiritual. We were at a crossroad.

Why did I stay? Why am I still here? Why didn't I leave? These are questions that I am sure every woman has experienced while fighting for her marriage. For me, prayer changed my life. And it can do the same for you.

In 2012, I began a daily prayer ministry that changed my outlook on my marriage, my life, and my relationships with others. It was a lifeline for me because I was drowning in these many different situations. Having a circle of prayer warriors made all the difference. When I began to take the focus off of my issues and began praying for others, I could see my solutions more clearly. Prayer gave me strength.

My outlook on life began to totally change, and I became hopeful again. This ministry birthed a new me. It helped me to love people for who they are, find the good in everyone, and understand that everyone is going through something.

As we got closer to getting our marriage in line and resolving long time issues, then here comes the enemy with an all-out attack and war on my family. This time it almost broke me. Something we had been working so hard for—a dream beginning to be realized, was all under attack. I had lost control and there was nothing that I could do to fix the situation. As a result, I decided that I couldn't take anymore and separation was the best decision at that moment.

My husband and I were apart for almost a year and during that time, it allowed us to deal with our demons. Anger, unforgivingness, selfishness—even a product of our experiences—we dealt with it all. We both sought professional help and I also sought professional help with a spiritual focus. We took baby steps to begin our healing and I was okay with that. My middle child was instrumental in facilitating forgivingness and I thank her for her strength and firm belief that *all things work together for good.* (Romans 8:28 KJV)

I saw my husband's efforts. He began to open up his Bible and read the Word. He started to send me text messages of how he could apply the Word to his life, his proof of sort. We would meet at church, attend services together, and even share in Sunday dinner. All the while, I continued daily prayer. I prayed that our relationship could be healed and that our family could be restored. I prayed that joy and happiness could return. I was praying for good things.

We made a decision to put our love first and choose marriage. Our love had produced three amazing kids all with greatness on the inside of them. Because we fought for our family, we showed our kids that there is nothing impossible for God. They have learned that you don't have to give up and call it quits when times get tough. I love our family. Love and life are worth working on. Our family is healing and whole because we decided to fight and not give up.

Decision to Choose Me

I'm glad that through the storms and rain that I endured in life, I was able to love me again. Although pregnant at age twenty-one, I loved *me* enough to finish my degree and graduate cum laude from FAMU. I am grateful that I chose a career in corporate America because it helped develop me into who I am today.

Early in my years in corporate, I gathered that I had a gift of gab. I understood that if I used this God-given gift, that it could open doors for me. In 2000, I resigned from a job in medical sales without another job lined up and was seven months pregnant with my second daughter. However, I just knew that there was something better in store for me. I went on a quest for what would be my dream job. Well, it didn't take long for me to find myself behind a desk interviewing with a Marriott hotel for a job in hospitality sales. As I shook hands with the general manager in my tight blazer attempting to cover up being seven months pregnant, I thought I'd better tell the truth about my pregnancy or jeopardize it all.

With the job offer in hand, I said to the general manager, "Before I sign this job offer, there is something that I have to tell you." She replied, "Sure, what is it?" I answered, "I am very excited about this offer and very excited about coming on board to make a difference at your hotel, however, I am seven months pregnant and will have to go on maternity leave shortly after beginning my position." Well, God just has a way of ordering our footsteps even when we don't know that that is what he is doing.

Needless to say, I got the job. Fifteen years later, that job in sales with Marriott opened up so many doors and led to so many promotions, awards, and accolades along the way. I have traveled to some of the best cities, stayed in the finest hotels, and ate some of the top cuisines.

But there was still this longing inside to use my gift of gab. I wanted more and I was in pursuit of something more, something different, and something more self-gratifying. My first encounter with that *something* was in 2004. I was invited by a friend to attend a women's conference. I was supposed to meet her there, so I jumped up early and got dressed in anticipation of being on time. I was just expecting to have a really good time hanging out. As I pulled into the parking lot, I received a message from my friend saying that she was not going to make it. I wasn't willing to turn around and go home. I was already there. I went inside and registered and what I saw on that stage was life changing—the keynote speaker! This lady came on stage with such fire, confidence, and energy. I sat on the edge of my seat knowing that this was the "it" I had been searching for.

I launched my speaking business in 2004, but for ten years I would struggle to get it off the ground. I made a few appearances with the launch of my brand, *NiaKay Enterprises*, but just never saw any real success. Sometimes it's all about timing and living a little more until you gain the necessary experiences to get you where you need to be. In January 2015, I relaunched my company and my brand. And a little more than a year later, I published my first book (which you are reading now) and accomplished even more.

I have literally had so many doors open for me in the area of speaking that I never dreamed possible. I have only scratched the surface. I have been the keynote speaker for the hospitality industry launch programs, new hire orientation for a very well-known daycare chain, Girls Inc., women's conferences, youth conferences, and much more. I am the creator and CEO of Everything Prayer Conference held annually on Dr. Martin Luther King, Jr.'s holiday weekend in Atlanta.

If you are reading this, know that everyone is going through something. No one is perfect—no relationship is perfect and no child is perfect. But if you just *decide* that quitting is not an option; jealousy is not an option; carrying guilt and condemnation about the past is not an option; hatred is not an option, and revenge is not an option, love is your only option. Take possession of your mind and believe in the infinite possibilities. Dream big! Change what you say concerning your life and your future. Understand that God loves you. You were made out of love. Love will propel you to your next level in life and love will save your family. Make a decision today to choose: to choose love, to choose you, and to choose life.

#SELFIE of Petrea Lovejoy

I was introduced to Petrea in the early 2000s by a mutual friend. At first glance, I thought we had nothing in common. Well, I probably even thought she was a little snooty. At the time, I really wasn't looking for any new friends and my life was in a good place. Little did I know how our relationship would evolve. Petrea is an extremely successful hairstylist on the south side of Atlanta. Her name is well-known and respected among colleagues and patrons alike. As she continued to expand her business and grow her brand, I began to take notice. My daughter, who is an up-and-coming artist, got to the point in her career where things were moving so fast that she needed a personal stylist—someone on speed dial. We both became Petrea's clients. It's this point in our relationship when I gained incredible respect for Petrea. As you read her jaw-dropping #SELFIE, you will do the same.

No Love Lost

At 10:30 a.m. on September 11, 2001, I was doing my last theory of school. It was my last day of cosmetology school when I heard the radio commentator say that the second building was hit. At that moment, I realized this was real. I knew I wasn't leaving school. On that day, the world changed and I knew that my life was changing too.

After I finished up that day, my mother said that I'd better go back to corporate which was in human resources. She figured I'd have more job security if I would return to the corporate world. At the time, I was married and had two young boys, but she thought that a consistent paycheck was more stable and a corporate job was safer. I was very successful in corporate America. I ran four temporary agency locations in Georgia. I hired and I fired and was good at what I did. My personality got me paid. When my mother said I should go back, my response was "No, they could never pay me what I am worth."

I remember her telling me one time that nobody is going to get their hair done. I also remember thinking that the only clientele I wanted to serve were the people who had a job. But as time went on, I started to pray for God to teach me and inspire me in doing hair. Two years later, I started to work at a very popular salon in Riverdale, Georgia. I was blessed to work next to a woman who taught me about hair. I appreciate her for teaching me about her craft. She even taught me how to advertise to a certain degree in our industry. God started to bless me, but little did I know, my home was about to be turned upside down.

I finally started to make money, but one day out of nowhere, I got a call from a neighbor who was also a hairstylist. I agreed to meet her at a restaurant, but little did I know, that meeting would change my life forever. I thought she wanted to meet about opening up a salon together, but I was wrong. She informed me that she overheard her husband talking and that my husband had another woman pregnant. At that moment, my heart dropped from my chest. I couldn't believe it. I drove home on two wheels (laugh out loud).

Once I arrived home, I told my husband what I'd heard and asked him if it were true. He said it wasn't, but I knew it was true. That night I couldn't sleep at all. The next day, I went to work tired and distraught. I even asked my sister if she thought that it was true. "Where there's smoke, there is fire," she said. And this particular sister is very naïve. Since I didn't want to believe it, I figured I'd asked her thinking that if she didn't believe it, I knew that I couldn't believe it either.

"Let's just go to the park and talk," I said to him. I remember it so well. That was the day my life changed. We were sitting in the car at the park. My youngest son was with us because we had to pick him up from school. I begged my husband to tell me the truth. But I knew the truth. He said, "Yes, I am so, so sorry." At that moment, my head started to spin. I blanked out. I just remember that the pain I felt was so unbearable. I remember pulling up to the house. The sun was out, but our house was shaded. I could barely climb up the stairs to my room. I sat on the edge of my bed and looked out of my window. I was numb to all the feelings. I asked God, "Am I dreaming? I want to wake up. Lord, I want out of this nightmare." I sat there and maybe ten minutes went by before my phone rang. It was a close friend from my place of worship, calling to say hey. I started to yell. "Please help me! Help me." She said, "I'm on the way."

When she arrived, she found me still sitting on the edge of my bed. She hugged me and told me that it would be okay. I remember her calling my sister to tell her to leave work. It was an emergency. She called my mom and my mom came right away too. By this time, my two sons were taken to a neighbor's house. My friend just held me. She told my husband to go ahead and leave because it was not safe for him to be there. He was crying and I was crying because of the pain that I was feeling. It was so unbearable. I remember my mom taking a black trash bag and just going in the dresser drawers and closet and pulling out his things. As she threw his things out of the house, my heart was hurting so bad. I remember my sister getting there. She started to cry with me. My friend said, "Let's go and get a drink." Keep in mind, I don't drink.

We went to a sports bar and I had a Coke. My friend said, "No baby, a drink. A glass of wine or something." We stayed there for about three hours—my sister, my friend, and I. I remember being there, but I was in a daze. I couldn't tell you what was being said. I just remember being like, *I want to wake up. I just want to wake up.*

That night was the hardest night of my life that I can remember thus far. I couldn't sleep, so my brother was at my house with me. He read the Bible to me the whole night. Every time he stopped reading, I would wake up. Then he would start back reading again. I didn't sleep for two weeks straight. I was so fatigued and tired.

As the weeks passed, I remember just breaking down at work. Before I knew it, three to four months had passed and my house was going into foreclosure. I remember the letter, but it didn't register that I wasn't paying my mortgage. Out of nowhere, I clicked back into reality and started to get a handle on my business. I so loved my husband and decided that we could work on the marriage.

"Don't do it. You will snap," my friend warned me. "I know you think you can handle what you are feeling, but you are going to snap." Six months later in the middle of the night, she was right. I snapped.

It was 3:13 a.m. and my eyes opened suddenly. I looked at my husband as he slept with both eyes closed as if everything was okay. He had the audacity to be sleeping like a baby, as I was feeling like someone had snatched my heart out of my chest, chopped it up, put it in a blender, and said swallow your heart again. I looked at the clock and said to myself, *He has five minutes to get out of here*. He had until 3:18 a.m. to be out.

First, I turned on the closet light. It shined on his face and he turned his back so the light wouldn't bother him. *Really? Really? Can you believe the nerve*, I thought. I went downstairs to our kitchen and grabbed a butcher knife. I sharpened it at least three times on the knife sharpener before slowly returning upstairs to our bedroom. I whispered in his ears, "Wake up.

Wake up. You have three minutes to get out of here or I will kill you." Then he woke up.

"Wait! Wait! Remember they said you may click. Let's just pray," he begged. I couldn't believe he could bring God into this after the pain he had caused me. "You are wasting time," I warned him. "You have one minute left to get out."

His reply was "No, you won't do it." That's what he thought. I took that knife and tried to stab him as he was lying in the bed. He moved and the knife went into the mattress getting stuck. By this time, he ran into the living room repeating, "Just pray. Please, let's pray." I replied, "Pray that your death is quick and easy." He ran into the guest room. He was behind the door pushing against it with all of his might. I had so much strength that I was able to open the door with one hand and try to stab him with the other. But he pushed the door on my funny bone while my arm was stretched around the door. All of a sudden, something came over me.

The tears ran down my face and all I could say to him was "Why? What could I have done to you to make you hurt me so bad?" As I slid down the opposite side of door, I just cried. "I am so sorry," he said. The rage over me was unbelievable, but calmness came over me, peace came over me. I jumped up, went to my car, and drove to my mom's house. "I was wondering how long it was going to take for you to break," she questioned. I didn't even remember to get my things from my house, so my mom went back and picked them up for me.

I stayed with my mom for about three weeks. At first, I had planned to move in with my mom for six months and then get an apartment. It was the first of the month and the mortgage was due. My husband couldn't pay the mortgage because he didn't have a job at the time, and I wasn't about to pay the mortgage. But my mom said, "Don't get rid of the house. Get rid of the man." I went home and ordered him to get out and go stay with his baby mama. I took back my home. From that point, the healing started, but I did cry for a while. At the beginning, I cried for weeks at a time, but I realized that as time went on I began to cry less and less.

    I decided to throw myself into my business. I was determined to be successful more than anything. Everything I desired came to my path. I spoke my future into existence. I eventually remodeled my home, purchased all new furniture, bought my first luxury vehicle, and scheduled maid services for my home. I was able to help my family members when they needed help. God poured all his blessings on me. I became a well-known hairstylist in the Atlanta area.

    As my sons grew older and wiser, my estranged husband would lie and tell them that he'd come get them. But he wouldn't come. Eventually, we dealt with that through therapy as individuals and even as a family. As time went on, my sons grew to be adults and both enlisted in the Navy. Through my experiences of marriage and love, God has shown me that he is love.

    After that trying experience, I thought I would never love again. Ten years later, I remarried. I vowed and prayed that I didn't ever want to love like *that* again. But somehow I opened up. I met a truck driver and we dated for a while. We lost contact for two years and in that time, I found out that I loved him.

    I remember talking to my sister and asking her how to get over someone who you love, someone who your heart is craving. She asked me to write down all the things I felt on a piece of paper such as if I had died today, what were the things I'd need him to know. She told me not to hold anything back. I wrote them down and burned the paper. I then went to my closet, got on my knees, and prayed for help. I asked the Lord to help me get over him. I didn't know how to find him. He was gone.

But then I decided that I was going to date *me* and no one else until I got over him. I wasn't going to date anyone else and however long it would take to completely get over him, well, that's just how long it would have to take. And I was willing to take the time. Keep in mind, my phone wasn't ringing. I wasn't giving out my phone number to anyone because my love continued to grow for this man. I made that decision on a Sunday. It was Tuesday or Wednesday of that same week when I got a random call. The voice on the line asked, "Who do you love? Please don't tell me you married that other guy!" He went on to explain how he had been trying to find me.

"Who is this?" I asked.

"Who do you love?" the voice repeated.

I said, "Andre."

He said, "It's me."

I thought, *Oh my God*.

I remember sitting in the parking lot of the gym telling him that I would not move my car without telling him how I felt, that if I had gotten into an accident and died, he would never know. This was my opportunity to tell him that I loved him with everything in me. He told me that he loved me too and had been looking for me. He was trying to remember my number and couldn't get it. "I have been dialing these numbers trying to find you," he explained. And from that moment, we reconnected. He found me and I found him. But little did I know that in two years, people change. While I was thinking he was the same, it was a fantasy.

We took turns going back and forth from Texas to Atlanta so we could see each other. He proposed to me with a four-karat diamond ring on my son's sixteenth birthday. We started planning and decided to get married in May 2012. I thought he was everything I had hoped for. He was different and he taught me to love again.

But then things changed. I didn't see any signs. I didn't see it coming. Four months into the marriage, he started cursing me out. He was the type of man who needed to be the provider, as most men feel they need to be, and was stressed about finances. Then all of a sudden, I came home with divorce papers because I couldn't handle the verbal abuse. Plus, I felt like I knew what would be next: physical abuse.

My husband's dad was a therapist and he referred him to a friend. We decided to go to counseling. Ironically, the friend was my youngest son's school counselor when I was going through my first divorce. That's how God works. My second marriage made me realize how important my relationship with my kids were especially because the counseling sessions started to help break down stuff. I found out that my husband had issues with his mother. He even flipped over the table during one of the sessions. I remember the counselor suggested that I may want to reevaluate our situation. He was familiar with what the first divorce had done to our family.

One day, we were having a regular argument at a red light (I don't even remember what the argument was about). He threw orange juice on me and spat on me. I froze. I was in shock. I didn't even know what to think. *Are you effin' crazy?* was something the Spirit said to me to stay calm. Then I started praying. "Lord, I can't do this. This can't be what I am in." I didn't say anything to anyone. No one knew of this incident. I swear I acted like it didn't happen. I erased it from my memory, swept it under the rug, and didn't address it.

It was the weekend of my class reunion when I decided to go out with my friends and co-workers—all of whom were married and on a curfew (2 a.m. was actually our cut off). I was at the sports bar and received a text from my teenage son. "You know your husband is stupid, right? he texted. "I just want you to know that your husband is outside the sports bar and I guess he thinks you are cheating or something."

Right outside of the sports bar was some patio furniture. He was sitting there with his legs crossed like he was going to catch me doing something wrong. My co-worker was there and everyone was walking out together. "Hey babe," I said, giving him a little kiss trying to play if off because I didn't want people to know that he had insecurity problems. But everybody could sense that something was wrong. My husband and I began to argue in front of the sports bar. He argued that it wasn't a class reunion and I argued that it was. "What do I have to lie for and who the hell are you? I said. "If I need to come out, I will come out."

This was a Saturday night. Sunday came and we weren't speaking at all. I was so mad that night that I slept in the guest room. The next day, we still didn't speak. It was Monday, August 29, 2011, and I had to go to work. His car wasn't working, so he took my car to help his family. We were texting and I told him that I had to go to work because somebody had to make the money. I knew it would hit him below the belt when I said that. He pulled up to the house expecting me to get in the car.

"I don't need you to drive me," I said. I got a license. I can take *them* home." He blurted out, "Get your butt in the car," I replied, "Get your behind out the car." He was in the car cursing me in front of his family, so I cursed him. He pulled off. I called a few friends and tried to get a ride, but couldn't find anyone. I thought he was going to stay gone, but the next thing I knew, he drove back to the house. As I was coming out the door, I had my phone, keys, and purse. He had the spare keys and got in front of me. "Man go on, just go on," I warned. He spat on me again, grabbed my phone, and threw it and my purse. "You don't believe they will take you to jail today, do you? Oh, you're going to jail!," I said. He argued, "I ain't going nowhere today."

My oldest son was in his room, but didn't know what was going on and my youngest son was at work. I asked my oldest son to borrow his phone so I could call the police and tell them about the assault. The police arrived and I had left the scene just like it was for them to see. It was a male police officer and he requested a female officer to join the scene. I remember calmly telling the police officer that he had spat on me. The officer said, "You've got to be joking." I informed him that I didn't even wipe my face—that he could swab the spit off of my face. My other girlfriend, who lived close by had pulled up. By that time, my husband was in the police officer's car and my son was asking what was going on.

My husband went to jail. I was crying and devastated. That's when I decided to tell everyone that this had happened before. I just didn't think it would happen again. They were shocked.

But this time I started to think that these incidents were getting closer and closer and I knew what was coming next. He was spitting on me, taking away all of my self-worth. I knew it would eventually get to a point when he would hit me and literally have me on the ground. I wouldn't even have the strength to get up because he would've had me mentally and emotionally bound. That's what abuse is and I didn't realize that that was what I was in.

We hadn't even been married fifteen or sixteen months by this time. He moved back in and I began a spiritual journey where I learned how to forgive. Forgiveness was my message. I tried to forgive him. We started going to church and marriage groups together, but he would never admit that any of this was his fault. He kept retelling the story and always made it seem like if "I hadn't made him mad … ." I would explain to him that he cursed me, that he needed to take responsibility for his actions, and if he couldn't take responsibility for his actions, he would do it again.

I would be like a sitting duck if he wasn't willing to take responsibility for his actions. His *I'm sorry* was more like, *Well, damn*. He acted like it was a white dress that he spilled red Kool-Aid on and could fix it by saying something like, "Well, okay I'll take it to the cleaners or I'll just buy you another one."

I remember one Tuesday night when he and my youngest son got into it. My husband was trying to make things hard for him. That night my son was on the back porch and he was listening to music. The volume was really faint. The crickets outside were louder than my son's music, but my husband yelled for him to turn it down. At this point, I knew he was picking at my son. I went on the back porch and was greeted with, "Mommy, you sure know how to pick them," my son stated sarcastically. "I sure know how to get rid of them too. Watch this. I bet when you come back home, I guarantee that he won't be here," I replied. I was talking loud and knew that my husband had heard me. I was to the point where if he didn't like it, he could get out.

On my youngest son's eighteenth birthday, we called it quits but not before my son got into one last argument with my husband. This particular night he had just got off from work. He came home and my son walked into my room. Talking low, my son pleaded, "Please tell him to leave my dog alone." My husband, who was sleeping in the guest room, came to my room going off. Everything happened in slow motion. My youngest son jumped in his face. "Oh, you gonna hit the dirt tonight. I am sick of you. You think we forgot about what you did to our Mama? I got you!" my son threatened. I jumped up, broke it up, and locked the door.

I heard the garage going up and my husband was about to leave in my car. I went down and asked him where he was going. "Don't worry about me," he replied and pulled off. Later, my husband came back home with the police and told his side of the story. "What was all the tension?" The police questioned, asking if I could add something more because it wasn't adding up. The officer didn't understand where all the tension was coming from and thought it wasn't anything. "He spat in my face," I shared. "Did the n-gga go to jail?" the officer replied. "Oh, he's been to jail," I reassured him.

The officer wanted to know when the divorce would be final because he didn't believe our marriage would work. By this time, another police officer had come and told my husband he couldn't stay there anymore, that someone had to go. My husband left, and that was his final exit. I remember that night he left. It was so peaceful.

I prayed to the Lord that if his heart was right to make me a more patient and forgiving wife. "If his heart isn't right, I need you to remove him from me. If you shall remove him Lord, then give me the strength to deal with it because I love him." I had been praying that prayer in silence. I knew he did something bad to me, but I still loved him. But I loved myself that much more.

I believe that there is always a breakthrough coming. Knowing the possibilities and knowing that you have not made it to where you are going, no matter how hard it appears to be—even when it's all or nothing, or I can't take it anymore, it's a breakthrough right there. What keeps me going? What motivates me? It varies. "I Am" is my affirmation. I am who I say I am. I run five days a week, five to six miles a day. When I run, the sweat, the pain, and all the negativity are released. I sweat off all of those things. Then I am ready for a new day. Every day I am always running to something.

But when hard times arise, I run through it and God gives me all of these great visions and directions as I run to it. Running for me has been cleansing. It helps me to see clearly. I started to focus on my business and threw myself into bettering myself. Through my experiences of inspiring women in my chair, I was shown my purpose in life. I was destined to be a motivational speaker, encouraging women, men, and children to do the best in life and to remember, "I am who I say that I am." I decided to dedicate my time to becoming a motivational speaker and started speaking at different women's conferences and speaking engagements in the hair industry. I also started speaking about the "I Am" theory. I opened up a very successful salon on the south side of Atlanta called D.O.V.E. (Daughters of Virtue and Excellence). My salon scripture is Proverbs 31 which speaks of the Virtuous woman. My first divorce was to show me that I will be a single parent, and my kids wouldn't want for anything. The second time around was about doubt and learning that I had to motivate myself. I also learned to watch who I was around. You have to be careful about who you associate with. You may even have to cut off family.

I hope that this story inspires you. If you are a single parent or just going through it, you are going to make it. It is always about perspective. No matter what is going on, I see the glass half-full. I don't take things for granted. Even when it feels like you don't have anything, be thankful for what you got.

#SELFIE of Nartasha Garcia

My very first run-in with Natarsha led me to believe that she was a know-it-all, "Perfect Patty." Little did I know, we had so many similarities in our #SELFIEs. Some connections are divine. Natarsha wears so many hats including minister. This lady is one of the most sought-after artistic directors in the Atlanta entertainment industry. For more than fifteen years, this remarkable and extremely successful woman has trained and developed superstars in the areas of singing, dancing, and acting. She is the CEO of AGI Entertainment, the premiere and elite artist development company dubbed as the New Motown and Natarsha, the next Berry Gordy! What I admire most about Natarsha is that she loves hard and is very transparent. The lives that she has impacted are in the thousands. When you read her #SELFIE, prepare to cry. But also prepare to learn how to dig down within and live again!

God Has a Plan

It has been said that God knows the end from the beginning. And I think God has a sense of humor that way. He forms us in our mother's womb. He places every desire, every dream in us. We think that when we come to Earth and are born, all these desires and dreams are our own. We have no idea that God's plan for us is to bring us to an expected end that he predestined even before we were born. We spend our lives trying to make our dream come true, not realizing that our dream is *his* dream, and that it will come to pass because it was the very reason we were created.

So my journey began at the age of four, when I realized I had been given a vocal gift. I didn't know where it had come from. I was too young to realize then that God had placed it in me. I didn't understand any of that. I just knew that I liked to sing.

I was ten years old when my mom took me to my very first concert. I didn't know what I was going to be seeing or hearing, but I sat on the edge of my seat in anticipation of whatever was going to happen in the next few minutes.

A ten-year-old girl was the reason this audience of some two or three hundred people had gathered. She sang several songs—five or so—then changed her clothes and came back onstage to sing several more songs. I was completely captivated. More than that, I felt like destiny and I had just met each other.

At the end of the concert my mom asked me what I thought of what I'd just seen and heard. Without hesitation, and with full conviction—even at my young age, I told her, "This is what I am supposed to do with my life."

Marching up to the mother of the young girl that had delivered such a powerful performance, my mother introduced me and told the woman that I'd made up my mind that I wanted to do just what her daughter had done that evening.

"Well, can she sing?" I remember the lady asking.

My mother admitted that she honestly wasn't sure. That she'd always thought of my efforts to sing as a lot of noise and that I'd been doing it since I was four years old.

They exchanged phone numbers that day and two weeks later I went on my very first audition. I didn't know *what* would happen that day. I didn't know *how* things would happen that day. I just knew that I was going to be a singer—that I was going to impact the world with my voice and that it was going to start with *this* audition on *this* day.

And it did! I performed well enough to be invited to be a part of the same concert I'd watched just weeks before. I had officially begun my journey, which eventually resulted in me signing my first record deal at age fifteen shortly after I won a local talent show. It would only get better from there. I was sure of it.

Singing became my priority but I did have one major distraction—a sweet boy I met and started dating when I was sixteen. He became my *second* priority and life suddenly became a lot more complicated. I started to rebel and do things my father didn't appreciate. We bumped heads more and more until one day he told me to get out of the house, to move out. I didn't understand why this man was so mad at me. I just didn't get it.

But he had demanded that I leave the house, so I did. I stayed with a family member briefly and it was then that I faced one of a few roadblocks in my life that could have destroyed me.

I found out that the father who I thought was my father *wasn't* my father.

In my head, I had always questioned whether my parents were really my parents. I didn't look like them. Their skin was darker than mine. From time to time, I would wonder whether I was adopted. My family assured me that I was not.

But this argument with my father that led to my leaving the house—this was huge. So much so that my family decided it was time to tell me the truth about the man I had known as my father all these years. The man who had raised me from the time I was one year old wasn't my real father.

It took some time to get over the hurt and pain of being lied to for sixteen years of my life. But I slowly began to understand his anger with me—what had led to this huge argument. He was disappointed that I didn't appreciate everything he'd been doing for me over the years—things I believed that he was supposed to do as my father. Only now I understood. He wasn't my father but he had lovingly taken on the responsibility anyway.

I have memories of my stepfather eating my vegetables off my plate when my mother turned her head. He would make sure I had money for lunch, and he would show up anywhere I needed him to be the super dad anytime I needed him. He went to work Monday through Friday providing everything our family needed and paying literally every bill like any loving father would.

Even still, I was only sixteen years old and at that age it was weird to learn that there was so much of the unknown in what I thought I'd known about my life. For instance, I wasn't the only child I'd always thought I was. I'd always wanted siblings and suddenly I had lots of them that I'd never known about. I learned that one of my mother's friends was really my aunt (my real father's sister). She lived in my hometown and she'd been keeping tabs on me for years and letting my dad know how I was growing up because he wasn't allowed to be a part of my life.

But God has his plan and he used the desire, the spirit he put inside of me, to turn this bad situation around. Because of him, I got to meet my real father. I got to know my real father and heal my real father who was feeling horrible that he wasn't a part of my life. Because of his plan, I was able to have a relationship to repair the breach—to meet my siblings, to gain more family the way I had always wanted to, and to become a part of what I now call my *huge* family.

Everything that happened during this experience taught me that hurt people *hurt people*—that sometimes not showing love doesn't necessarily mean that a person doesn't want to love. It's that they don't know *how* to love. It gave me compassion for fathers and mothers who don't raise their own children. And in this business that I now own where I work with children who have personal and family issues, and are in crisis, I can see it from both sides because I lived it.

God had his plan for me. And he wasn't done.

Three years later, at the age of nineteen, I experienced yet another major roadblock: an unexpected pregnancy.

I was the popular girl in my hometown. Kids looked up to me and wanted to be like me. Except now I was the girl with the scarlet letter. I was no longer that role model. Instead, I was an unwed pregnant teenager and the parents of those kids who had once looked up to me no longer wanted their children anywhere near me—as if being pregnant was a disease their kids could catch from me.

I thought my life was over. I had disappointed the town. I had disappointed my mom. And I had disappointed my dad—though he didn't say much to me at that time. He had been diagnosed with cancer and was suffering through that terrible illness and the difficult treatment program that came with it I had disappointed everyone.

I retreated to my bedroom and spent a lot of time there alone. There were many tears, but no prayers. I couldn't talk to God. I felt like I had let him down too.

It affected how I interacted with people. When they whispered, I assumed they were talking about me except they weren't saying good things. So, I talked *myself* up and said good things about me because I knew nobody else would.

I sought and found deeper friendships and one came in the form of my boyfriend's mother. It was as though God had placed her in my life to love me through this process. She bought my maternity clothes. She drove me to appointments. She took me out to dinner. She did a lot of things with me that no one else would do and to this day we are still very close.

Most of the people I had grown up with were away experiencing college life by now—the life I had always envisioned for myself. In fact, I'd always wanted to go to a school in New York and had dreamed of making the same plans they had. But, it wasn't going to happen that way. I was told by my father that I should either go to school or have the baby. I wasn't encouraged to do both nor did I think I could. I decided to have the baby and I took classes at a community college. While all my friends were away at school, I was at home being the disappointment. This was the hardest point of my life. I didn't think I would ever wake up from this nightmare.

A little girl came up to me once and told me she wanted to be just like me. I remember thinking, *Do I really want her to be like me?* Because even though I had a gift that could inspire people and I was spreading the good news, I was pregnant now. Life was no longer the same. People were treating me differently. I wasn't invited to sing anywhere anymore. My stepfather didn't want to look at me.

I began to wonder if I should even have this baby.

My mother didn't wonder, though. Yes, she was disappointed in me, though I realized over time that her disappointment wasn't just about me getting pregnant. It was also about all the lies that *led up to* me getting pregnant. She believed me when I said I wasn't sexually active. "I don't like boys like that," I would tell her. And she believed me. She defended me when people told her things about me and the things I was doing. She dismissed their talk as mean gossip. I think the image of me in her head was of this daughter who was honest and who wouldn't do any wrong. To learn that I hadn't been truthful with her was the bigger disappointment, I think.

But when my mom turned the corner and decided she would support me, she was *all in* with me all the way. She was proud of me. She stood by me firmly.

I absolutely love my mother! She is a dear heart, probably one of the sweetest people on the planet that I know. She loves me ferociously. She made sacrifices for me that I only later came to understand.

For instance, she was married to her husband *for me*. She didn't want me to grow up in a single-parent home and she didn't think she could take care of me by herself. When the man who would later become my stepfather came into her life and began to take care of me, babysit me, and bring diapers and food for me, my mother made the ultimate sacrifice. She married this man when he proposed because she knew that he absolutely loved *me*. I don't even know if he loved her as much and she definitely didn't experience the love she deserved. She didn't care. She wanted a man around that loved her daughter. That was most important of all.

She stayed with him for me too—even through the bad times. My stepfather was overall a good man and he provided for us, yes. But even as he did so, he was dealing with a lot of demons. Alcohol was one of them. He was one person throughout the week and on the weekends—because of his heavy drinking—we would watch him turn into someone completely different. My mom and I never knew what to expect when he came home. We constantly lived on pins and needles.

When my son was born, I named him Brandin. My stepfather finally came around. He was very supportive. He loved Brandin. I had moved out shortly before giving birth and times were hard. So, my stepfather let Brandin and I move back into the family home and he was genuinely happy to have us there.

We had our difficult times over the years, my stepfather and I. But, I didn't want to dwell on all the bad things he had done. He was dying. Instead, I focused on all the *good* things he'd brought to my life. All I had ever wanted was to make him proud of me.

And although he is no longer here, I believe that he is extremely proud of me in Heaven. My father accepted Jesus on his deathbed in the hospital. At that time, I didn't really know how important that was because I wasn't where I personally needed to be with Christ. But now that I truly understand God's plan. I know that my stepfather (my father) is a part of that cloud of witnesses in Heaven watching me and rooting me on in my life even now. And I know I will see him again.

It has been twenty-four years since he passed. I look back now and I realize it was at that time that my mother started living. Not that I wanted my stepfather to die, But after he did, I saw the chains break free from my mom, who I believe lost out on a lot because of the decisions she made to marry and stay with him no matter what—for me. I watched her begin to do the things she'd only ever dreamed of doing because she no longer had to bear that heavy load.

My mother is thriving now! She is a part of our business. She supports me in everything I do. She is always there with me on important occasions. In fact, she's there for my beautiful son, Brandin the very same way. He may have been unexpected but he was never unwelcomed, especially by my mother. She was Nana from the time he came out until even now—no matter what.

Her relationship with me and Brandin is a bond that will never be broken. It's our goal in life—his and mine—to take care of her in her best years (which I don't believe she has even lived yet). She is my little sweet thang and I love her unconditionally.

I thank God regularly even now for her words and her support. Because little did I know then—through the dark and difficult days of my youth—that my son would be the biggest blessing to my life. The biggest part of God's plan for me. Had I not made the choices I made and ended up in the place I was in, I don't know that Brandin would be here.

Understand: I don't condone premarital sex and having children out of wedlock. But I want to encourage people who think that having a child before you are married means your life is over. God has a plan, and his plan for your life is going to happen regardless of what you do. And even when we make mistakes in our life, there is a redemptive process in the mistake to get us back on the road to where we need to go.

Any moms with daughters who make mistakes and find themselves pregnant, don't turn your back on them. Continue to love them the same way God loves all of us. Forgive them, let it go, and support them through their challenging days.

And be encouraged. *Weeping may endure for a night, but joy comes in the morning* (Psalms 30:5 KJV), so just hold on. You will laugh again. You will smile again. You will love again.

God knows the beginning from the end. And I saw that demonstrated once again when it came to my finding true love. As a young girl, I had—like any other young girl—dreamed of the day I would meet my Prince Charming. I took it a step further than just dreaming, though. I began to put together a box of goodies I thought the husband I would someday have would want. If I was in the store and saw something I thought he might like, I would buy it. Over time, I'd filled this box with all sorts of treasures for the husband-to-be that I hadn't even met yet. Cards, shirts, mugs—anything I imagined he would like. I was that sure in my mind that God was going to bring this man into my life.

And that man did eventually come. But I'll tell you this, if I hadn't had my eyes open, I would've missed him! He didn't show up looking at all the way I thought he would.

I met him one day at a small church where I happened to be singing that day. After the service, he approached me, introduced himself as Craig, and asked me for my autograph.

"I will surely give you my autograph, but I don't think I am who you think I am," I remember saying.

It took him a moment to realize that I indeed was *not* who he thought I was—a member of an R&B group he later admitted. He was clearly a little embarrassed but we broke up the awkward moment with laughter. That was the beginning of our conversation. And the beginning of a platonic friendship.

Platonic because Craig was dating someone else at that time and had just moved to Atlanta. I invited him and his girlfriend over to have dinner with me and my son. We had a great time and our friendship continued to blossom over time.

I learned that he was on his personal journey to finding Christ. He hadn't grown up in the church and he didn't really know anything about Jesus. He had been invited to that particular church where we met on that particular day by someone who was the trainer at this security company. Ironically, I worked at the same company and was invited to that same church by that same person! I was from Connecticut, Craig was from Massachusetts, and we'd been living three hours away from each other all our lives. Yet, God had brought us all the way down to *Georgia* to meet each other. Crazy.

Craig and I became really close friends. We studied the Word together, went to church together, and hung out together. He and his girlfriend eventually broke up and Craig and I decided that we would just practice submission for each other in order to be prepared for whoever God was going to bring into each of our lives. He opened doors for me. I cooked for him. We shared dishwashing duty. He treated me how he would treat the wife God was going to give him and I treated him how I would treat the husband God was going to someday give me. Every now and then we would wonder out loud if God meant for *us* to be together. We would always laugh and we decided he hadn't.

I kept on praying to God to send my husband. There were times I could swear that I would hear him ask me if I had considered Craig—that everything I was praying for, he was putting into Craig and didn't I see that? I said, "no."

But I approached Craig about it one day asking him if God was giving *him* any word about me in any way. He said, "no."

We went on that way for a while—both of us denying how God was dealing with the two of us in relation to each other and Craig was actually babysitting my son as I went out on dates with other men! Little did I know, God *was* talking to Craig about me—that Craig would ask Him to show him his wife and God would tell him, "Look up."

"That's just Tarsha," he would say in reply to God as he looked up and I'd be standing there. "Is there somebody behind her because clearly you aren't talking about her."

We played this game for about eight months with God speaking to both of us and both of us denying it to ourselves and to each other.

And then we were at church one day. It was New Year's Eve. The pastor was preaching and saying things like, "Now is the time to enter the year," "God is calling you to do certain things," "You need to stop procrastinating," and "It's time to move into your destiny."

"Marry me," Craig said to me suddenly, right there in the middle of the pastor's sermon. I didn't respond. I couldn't! I just sat there for the rest of the service with my mouth hanging wide open. I didn't answer him until afterward.

We had never dated and we had only ever been friends. But when he asked me, it was like the stars aligned. Everything was right there, right then, and we both *knew*.

"*Oh my God, we have to tell everybody!*" was our next thought. After all, everyone only knew us to be friends. So, we approached the pastor and Craig told him that he'd asked me to marry him.

"About time," was his response. "You didn't know, but we all knew."

God had already ordained it. We were married four months later on April 4, 1998, and we've been married for eighteen years now. Eighteen years of practicing submission, enjoying each other's company, and being best friends without ever even going on an official date. We went from friendship to engagement to marriage—the best decision I have ever made in my life.

And, yes ladies, he did get the box of treasures that I'd been filling for my husband-to-be all those years. And he got the box that God had been preparing for him—me! I got my gift as well. My husband, my Prince Charming, has proven to be the biggest gift God has ever sent down from Heaven to me. All of the things I have ever gone through in my life—good, bad, indifferent—was all worth it. God wrapped a man in flesh to handle me and to love me unconditionally. To accept me, flaws and all. To inspire me to bring out the best in me.

The Bible talks about husbands washing their wives with the waters of the Word. My husband does that. God wrapped a man in flesh to repair the grief in my heart, to be the father I've never seen, the husband I never witnessed, the man of God that I never even dreamed of having because I didn't know it was possible. God wrapped a man in flesh to have eyes only for me. To never call my son *stepson*—only *son*.

I know that God sent him for me. Everything that I am, everything I want to be, everything I dream of doing before I leave this earth—he has inspired me to do. It was never just about singing. It had everything to do with impacting the world and changing lives.

My husband is an entrepreneur. He has always had businesses. At age thirteen, he was the guy who brought candy to school and sold it in the hallways. He was the soda man with the sodas. He had a cleaning business, a music-related business, an organizing business—all kinds of businesses, and all before the age of nineteen. I never wanted to have a business. I never dreamed of owning a business. All I wanted to do was sing. But God brought an entrepreneur together with a dreamer so that we could change the world. Every dream that Craig ever had, I was the missing piece needed to put legs to it. Craig had the dream but he didn't have the details. I helped him figure out those details and together we were armed to change the world the way God wanted us to.

The Bible says that God will give you the desires of your heart. Those desires are ones he placed in you. He gave me a desire for my husband and he gave my husband a desire for me so that we could find one another, come together, and change the world.

I encourage every young girl out there that has her treasure box to keep filling it with things for that husband-to-be, for that man that is coming someday! Keep your eyes and your heart open. He may come in the form of the guy you pass all the time in the grocery store that you thought was just the "grocery store guy." He may come in the form of a friend that you would never think would be your husband. And what could be better than marrying your best friend?

This best friend and I now own a business that is thriving. We mentor couples. We oversee a church. We have ten godchildren. We have hundreds of clients that are also our children (Craig and I have never had our own together. I sometimes teasingly claim that my mother cursed me after I had my son because she didn't want me to keep having children), and we just love to be a blessing to people. We have big dreams that involve other people. Our biggest one is to buy a house for someone who needs it. To purchase a car for someone who needs one. To pay someone's grocery store bill before they even get to the register. We find ways to be a blessing because we love to see people experience God's love in action. It is so undeniable and we want other people to wake up every day the same we way do—with new mercies.

The sun, the sky, the birds, the trees, the moon—all made by God. We ourselves are wonderfully made! So much that if you're like me, you too look at yourself and question who you are that God would be so mindful of you that he knows even the number of hairs on your head and the pain in your heart. Surely, he didn't create any of us just to take up space. Surely, he didn't create any of us to become nothing, or to not matter to ourselves or someone else.

I believe he created us to solve problems. The problems that I am going to solve and the problems that you are going to solve are going to be whatever problems *he* created us to solve. Yours may not be the same as mine. But rest assured that there *is* a problem that you were specifically created to solve. Perhaps it is to give more love or to put smiles on the faces of strangers when you walk in the grocery store. There's a reason you were created. You do matter. There are no throwaways in his kingdom.

So, I need you to pull up your boot straps and go look at yourself in the mirror and say out loud, "I am fearfully and wonderfully made and God has a plan for my life." If you have to tell yourself that every day until you believe it, then that's what you do. God has a plan for your life, my friend. Your dream and your passion—whatever it is that is bubbling on the inside of you—is only the vehicle to get you there. It's the vehicle to get you started on your journey. Remember, mine started when I sat in that church and saw that girl singing. That was the vehicle. I jumped in that vehicle then and I've been riding ever since.

I look at where I am now and I can honestly say that I am no longer trying to figure out my purpose. I know what it is—to help other people see the fulfillment of their dreams. That is the purpose for which I was created. As I look back over my life and connect the dots, it's perfectly clear what my purpose was meant to be all along and that God always had a plan.

We are imperfect. We all make mistakes. But, God can put a blessing even in the mistakes! My pregnancy was unexpected—the result of mistakes I made in my life. But, the very presence of Brandin brought everything God wanted me to have in my life and gave me the answers to every problem that I have—even now, twenty-six years later. God created mankind and thought of every error that could be made and he has a redemptive plan in every one of those errors. No need to dwell on or worry about what our lives are going to look like or if we have ruined our lives beyond repair.

Take a girlfriend of mine, for instance. Her son got himself into some trouble and went to jail. She called me one day in tears about the situation. I reminded her about Joseph and how God had made him a king in jail. I assured her that God was protecting her son's life. That God had put him there to keep his lifestyle from claiming his life and to someday make that young man a king—either while he is in jail or after he comes out (*his* plan).

A pilot flies a plane but he doesn't do so alone. There is a course-correction mechanism in place the entire flight to keep that plane heading toward its intended destination. A degree off-course to the right or to the left and that mechanism kicks in to bring the plane back to safety and heading in the right direction. That is how God guides our lives.

Look at every obstacle that life will throw at you and just remember that you have a silent partner working on your behalf who you don even see and who is fixing things for you—things of which you don't even know. Course correction.

God has a plan and if you just trust his plan, you won't have to get up every day worrying. The Bible tells us that *he feeds the fish and the birds, and he clothes the trees* (Matthew 6:26 NLT). Surely he has our lives figured out. All we have to do is walk in destiny. And if we do that, we can live the best life ever.

#SELFIE of Natasha Cozart

All I can say about this amazing woman is "Wow!" A single mom of six children with an amazing body, Natasha is extremely disciplined, organized, and has established herself as a marketing guru and parenting expert. We too had a mutual acquaintance who merged our business relationship and growing friendship. Our relationship is the newest, but I continue to be amazed at her strength and tenacity to go on. Life will throw you some curve balls, but your attitude will determine your altitude. What I love about Natasha is that she does not wear her life or circumstances on her sleeve. She is not having a pity party but is busy building her brand and leaving her legacy. This #SELFIE is full of drama, which I know you will love. It is also uplifting and encouraging, and it definitely will leave you feeling like, *If she can do it, so can I*.

Six Feet Deep

I woke up early around 5 a.m. because that was the only time I could enjoy the silence. Having given birth to five children, ages eight and under, and with baby number six on the way (more about that later), the *Mama* song gets played on repeat. You know the song. It's the tune your kid sings when they're clearly busy in another room, but they're still demanding your attention.

Needless to say, I was playing with a full deck of cards and each of my children were aiming for the jackpot. Whether I was resolving a communication conflict, recovering missing toys, kissing a boo-boo, cooking a meal, performing my wifely duties (you know what I mean), or taking one of my many prenatal visits to the restroom, there's no other way to put it. My life was one big barrel of overwhelm and I was drowning, sinking in despair.

To make matters worse, I hadn't been out of the house in over five days. You see, earlier that week I was scheduled to attend a retreat which I had planned three months in advance. But unexpectedly at the last minute, my husband had other plans and wasn't able to stay home to watch the kids. I was so isolated and depressed that I felt I would never be free to truly live again. It never crossed my mind to hire a babysitter, because I didn't have the money and I didn't have any friends.

That's why it was vitally important that I intentionally spent some quiet time in prayer and reading every day. This was my formula for saving the last bit of sanity I had left and it had worked pretty well up to this point. So, that morning I prayed and read as much as I could—with light naps in between—until the kids woke up around 8 a.m. Then I made them breakfast, but not without first having to clean up the mess in the kitchen that was left over from dinner the previous night. My husband said he was going to take care of it, but never did. This really frustrated me because my goal was to spend the bulk of that day tackling the mountain of dirty clothes that I could never seem to make a dent in. Instead, I'd spent half the morning cleaning in the kitchen. I could feel my blood beginning to boil, but I was able to suppress the negative feelings with recent memories of a fleeting peace during my quiet time of meditation a few hours earlier.

As you could expect, by the time my husband woke up around noon, the blood boil had matured into a full-blown fire in my heart. I was angry about a lot of things, more than just the dirty kitchen. I was angry because even though we had been living with my mother for the past five years, the unemployed man who asked me not to work—even though I could easily land an executive position— was not awake during peak business hours actively looking for a job. He was just rolling out of an early afternoon stupor.

I was especially angry with myself for getting pregnant, again! I'm embarrassed to admit it, but that's the truth about where I was during that time. I was three months into a pregnancy by a man who I knew neither loved me, nor respected me. And even though he was also my husband, I knew the facts would never ever change. I was angry because I watched his mother, who was dying from cancer, living in the exact same situation for more than thirty years. I wondered how she could live with such marital disrespect, blatant infidelity, and emotionally abusive cruelty for so many years while still serving her family and community with a smile as if nothing were wrong. I was angry because I knew that she would probably die without ever receiving the love, respect, and honor she deserved. An apology would have also been nice.

With those issues weighing on my mind, I wanted to scream for her and for myself. I decided right then and there that her story would not be *my* story. I wanted to be "sixty and sexy" like the international supermodel Beverly Johnson, not "sixty and suffering" from a terminal illness. Furthermore, I didn't want to be the woman who wears the perpetual mask, pretending her life is perfect for the sake of religious affiliations. Honestly, I had no idea what I was going to do to change my current situation, but I did know that I'd reached the point of no return with a clearer view of my reality than I'd had the previous day.

Above all, I knew that I didn't want to see my daughter endure the same negative cycles of abuse, infidelity, and mistreatment as the two previous generations. When their dad walked into the room, the kids immediately came to attention and welcomed him because I've always taught them to honor the presence of their father no matter what he's done to me. I did this hoping that even if he were unworthy, there would be a presence of hope in the eye of the children reflecting the man he could become. After all the good morning hugs had been exchanged, my husband did something that he normally didn't do. When he's hungry, he would normally just go to the refrigerator, get whatever he wanted, and make his own meal. This time instead of doing his normal routine, he turned and asked me a question. He said he had a taste for bacon and asked did I want him to make some.

Now this may seem like a harmless question, but if you know anything about cooking bacon, you know that it can be a very messy experience. Bacon makes a lot of grease in the frying pan and that grease gets all over the countertops and everything else within a mile radius. Now, I must give him the benefit of the doubt. If he'd known what mental state I had been in for the past six hours, he might have chosen to continue with his infamous silent treatment. He hadn't been speaking to me for the past couple of days because he wanted to prove a point when I pissed him off about something.

Here's something I realized during the first year of marriage. When you're married to someone who's a talker, getting them to shut up for a few minutes is actually a bit of a challenge, let alone silencing them for multiple days in a row. I know I shouldn't say this, but as a part-time introvert, I can honestly admit that I enjoyed getting the silent treatment. I would even find myself secretly doing things to piss him off, hoping to get a few days off from ear duty. When he asked me the loaded bacon question, I had just finished transforming the kitchen into a makeshift laundromat. The counters were clean because I needed them to fold and organize the once dirty, now newly cleaned clothes that I didn't want to wrinkle. If I barely had time to wash the dirty clothes, there was no way that I would have time to iron wrinkled clothes. Since I didn't respond the first time, he asked me again if I wanted him to cook some bacon and eggs. Again, this may not seem like a loaded question. But after you've been in the kitchen cleaning up and you're always the one who gets to clean up no matter who's doing the cooking, plus, you're three months pregnant and you're already mad at him, you already know this situation is about to blow up. If I had learned any Godly virtues during my quiet time that morning, now would have been the perfect opportunity to show them. But the situation was beyond repair. My heart longed for answers, for results, for change. At least I can say that I started out on the right track.

Looking back, I should have declined his offer to avoid the pursuing conflict. Instead, I responded with as calm a voice as I could manage, accepting his offer with the one stipulation that he would do the cleaning once it's all done. He was immediately offended, but I didn't care. He tried to remind me of all the few times that he'd cleaned the kitchen, but none of that mattered. He hadn't cleaned up the night before and at the present, I needed my new laundry-kitchen to be squeaky clean. His offense and my anger were catalysts for an instant argument. You know the ingredients: a pinch of blame, 1/2 teaspoon of denial, 1 cup of accusation, 3 gallons of self-defense. Mix together with increasing decibels until it explodes. He got so mad at me that he began to pack his bags and storm out of the house.

Note: I don't recommend doing what I did next. This sort of thing only works in the movies and is classic bad behavior. As he stormed out of the house, I went behind him pressing for anything that resembled responsibility and honor, but I came up empty and even more convinced of my pending transition.

By this time, the kids heard the commotion and were coming to investigate. That's when the tables turned. He began to use the kids against me. Apparently they had been listening through the door and heard him repeating the question about making bacon. His demeanor completely changed and they sided together against me. At that point, I withdrew from engaging further in the discussion. That blow was beneath the belt. The number one rule for parental arguments is to never involve the kids because they should never feel the pressure to honor one parent over the other. They were too young to understand the gravity of marital accountability.

By then I just wanted the conversation to be over, so I apologized. But it was too late. He was already perched on his preaching soapbox and I was going to get another dreadful lecture about a woman's role and responsibility in marriage. I listened for a moment. Then I interrupted with a question of my own. I asked him if he was ever planning to get the marriage counselor for us. I'd been asking him to do this for a few years so we could work on peeling back the many layers of crap that we were calling a marriage. But he never had.

Since we both had calmed down, I figured we could try to talk things through and finally decide on a marriage counselor. It was painfully obvious that our relationship was in disrepair. Actually, I tried to get us some counseling a year prior, but he would not cooperate with exercises and he eventually quit attending his sessions. Fortunately for me, I continued my sessions which is why I finally found a backbone to stand up on. Nothing could have prepared me for what would happen next. It was like the reverse-loaded-bacon-question. When he didn't answer the first time, I should have seen it coming, but I didn't. The second time I asked, he turned and looked me in the eye to make sure I got his message. His answer was a resounding NO! No, he had not found a marriage counselor and he would never hire a marriage counselor to tell him what he already knew, because according to him, there was nothing wrong.

For some reason, this statement coupled with his fierce gaze hit me like a ton of bricks. For the first time, I could see the forest as well as the trees. From that point onward, it was like I had an out-of-body experience. I could see myself sitting at the table, but it wasn't the me who I knew. The woman sitting there was depressed, worn out, and on the verge of a nervous breakdown. Immediately my mind began racing with questions looking for more answers:

How long had I been living under this harsh oppression?
What did I do to deserve this?
How much longer should I be expected to accept mistreatment?
If anything happened to me, would anyone even notice?
What good was my life?
What purpose did I even serve (outside of sexual favors, baby-machine, and housekeeping—jobs that could easily be outsourced)?

For the first time, I saw a woman who was being used for her body. I was nothing more than a prostitute and a slave except I didn't get paid, and I was responsible for providing all resources for living.

For some reason, that last *no* just woke up something in me. It was like I finally knew that if I didn't do something, I would never ever survive this. It was the fight or flight instinct. I knew he cared nothing about me, cared nothing about our marriage, and all was already lost. You would think that I could've seen that before, but I just didn't.

If you have been trapped underwater for a long time, you don't recognize when it's raining outside because everything around you is already wet. That's how I was. For the first time, I was able to step outside of myself and see my situation for what it really was. The abuse would never stop; the lies would never stop; he would never help with daily chores; he would never get a decent job; he would never take financial responsibility; and I would never be able to follow my dreams, not as long as I was in this current situation.

I stepped so far out of my body and out of myself, that the next part that I'm about to tell you was seriously an out-of-body experience. This would probably be the first time I can honestly say I know I flipped out. I guess the technical term for this would be a panic attack, but the realization struck me like a thousand pounds and it crushed me. But instead of huddling in a corner and crying my eyes out, I got very angry at him and at myself mostly for letting this happen, for not having the insight beforehand, for letting my children see me being treated this way, and actually for even having children at all and bringing them into a world of emotional and physical abuse.

I immediately knew that I had to get out of there and get away from him. I needed to clear my head and think. But this man reached into the car through the passenger side window just as I was going around to the driver side, and took the car keys out of the ignition. I ran outside, but as you already know, it was early in the morning and I wasn't properly dressed. I hadn't showered or combed my hair in days, so you can imagine what I was looking like—a ratchet mess! By this point, I was sobbing uncontrollably. I just started walking up the street, but since I could barely see through the tears, it took me a moment to realize I was going the wrong way. We lived in a cul-de-sac and the route I was taking was just going to lead me right back home.

All the while, he was following me, taunting me, "What are you going to do? Get back in the house! You ain't gonna do nothing!" Then I would shout back, "Shut up talking to me! I hate you! You don't love me! You don't care nothing about me! I don't have to take this!" As I turned around to walk in the other direction, I realized that I lived too far away from any main roads to get anywhere helpful and our neighborhood didn't have access to public transportation. I was so angry because in a way, he was right. What was I really trying to accomplish? I had no clue. I didn't have an exit strategy. I had no plans in place. I had no job, no money. I only knew that I couldn't stay in the situation I was in for one moment longer.

It all seems kind of comical now. But at the time I just needed an out. I calmed myself down as much as I could and went inside the house. I called everybody I could think of until one person answered and was willing to come get me. I kissed my kids and told them Mommy loved them, but there were going to be some changes when I returned. Then I very calmly picked up my purse and went to sit on the porch awaiting my ride. That was the last day we were ever together as one big, messed up family.

As I reflect on the situation, I've wondered many times what did I do wrong. I thought I was married to the right person. I thought I used wisdom in every situation and even after I knew the situation was messed up in our marriage, I prayed and prayed and prayed, but he never changed and the situation never changed. What was the breakdown? I just needed to know how to move forward by understanding my mistakes from the past.

As I was reading a very good book by my life coach and mentor, I realized that I had given away my personal power. I had given him the right to treat me in whatever way he wanted to because I never valued my own worth or my own identity. We were married for eleven years, and I was pregnant or either nursing a baby for the entire time—even after we were separated.

It wasn't until we were separated that I finally learned to call for help meaning 9-1-1 or legal intervention. You never get used to looking into the eyes of someone that you love as they manhandle you or threaten to kill you. Unfortunately, the years spent in isolation away from my family and only focused on my husband had left me with no life of my own. Every time I would leave the house, he would accuse me of infidelity. Every time he knew I was talking to a male colleague on the phone, he would accuse me of misbehavior. I had literally spent years learning to adapt to mistreatment; learning to live without money, without meaningful friendships (unless he approved); never expecting anything for myself, and I was completely overwhelmed. And that's the thing that drives people to a ratchet lifestyle and inappropriate behavior.

As mentioned in my book *Ratchet Mom*, when people are stressed out, overworked, underpaid, and emotionally spent, they do strange things that are vastly inappropriate. But I'm acknowledging that it is mostly a cry for help.

I don't know your specific situation, but I do know that you have the power to bring change into your own life. You cannot fear what people will say about you or think about you, especially if you're a Christian woman or even a preacher's wife.

Every week you can comb the news and find stories of leaders, inside and outside of the church, who have misused their influence to molest, rape, or mistreat women and children and it's wrong. A public figure can create an external persona that clearly misrepresents their true nature. It's very ironic that people don't want to believe women when they come forward about abuse. What mother and wife in her right mind have ever had the desire to make up abuse allegations?

When people act like they don't believe me, I'm reminded about the two or three recent years that I'd been home weeks and months at a time with no babysitters, almost losing my mind and being severely depressed. How the heck do you think I had time for an affair when I didn't even have time for a shower? I've grown past what people say and think about me. And furthermore, I don't care who believes me or not.

At first, I used to cry and wonder, *Why don't they believe me?* And then I realized that if you want to live in a world of manipulation and deception, that's on you. I want to know the truth and only live in the truth no matter what. And if you're suffering silently at the hands of a leader because you're trying to protect his reputation, Sweetie, you will suffer all your life and no one will know. And here's the hard truth—they don't care. You have to take care of yourself and get yourself some help.

I was devastated during the first year after my separation because the majority of the people who I thought were my family and friends had been poisoned by lies. Instead of extending love and acceptance to me, seeking to find the truth, or simply staying out of it, they rejected me. I was super close to my ex-husband's brother and his wife because they mentored me during my last years of college. I thought they would be there for me, but I was wrong about them and about a lot of other people. I'm good about reading people's vibes and I know when someone has been talking about me. I could tell when my ex- had been to the school spreading lies to the teachers. I had to develop tough skin.

Normally I am very sensitive to what people say and how they feel about me. I used to have this huge desire to be understood and accepted, but I've grown to the point where I don't let other people's opinion of me have an affect on my opinion of myself. Yes, I'm aware of what they think, but I choose not to engage them or internalize their vibes. I let it bounce off and I keep moving toward my destiny.

The most fulfilling thing I have been able to do in the past few years is getting a clear sense of my identity and knowing the reason why I exist on the earth. I know that I'm a natural-born giver and fixer. That's why I was attracted to a broken man. I could see his potential and I believed in what he could become. But it's not enough to believe in someone if they don't believe in themselves. If they will never put action to their words, there will never be any change or development of that potential and you will forever be disappointed by the unplanted seed.

I know it's my purpose in life to be there for other women. We have so much riding on our shoulders, and we're so full of potential. Think of how much more powerful we will become if we unite forces and support one another. I can't judge you for where you are because I've been there too. I can't look down on your hardships, weaknesses, or expressions of "ratchetness" because I've had mine too. I can't gossip about your baby daddy drama because I still have drama going on in my life too.

My purpose is to share light and hope every chance I get. I started a blog to publicly express my gratitude to those who I've had the pleasure of meeting along my path of discovery in hopes that others could be encouraged and filled with light while traveling along their own destiny road in life. We are a team. My blog, TeamNatasha, is about finding, keeping, and enhancing your authentic identity. I firmly believe that all people have a God-given purpose for existence and the journey toward discovering and actuating that destiny is the sum total of individual decisions—that's what we have in common. Each decision affords us the opportunity to meet new people, garner wisdom from their experiences, and collectively grow together.

Of all the decisions I've made, the most important and life-changing was making Jesus my Lord and Savior. I used to be very shy and insecure, searching for my life's meaning through unhealthy relationships. But human error and countless disappointments drove me to look within for the peace that could only be found in God. Now every other decision in my life is filtered through that lens—through the filter of faith.

As a result of having earned two masters' degrees, I have had the opportunity to sharpen my skills in many various disciplines. I started my own marketing agency where I service businesses and organizations with marketing and strategic growth strategies. For over fifteen years, I have worked directly with the top brands in personal, spiritual, and professional development. I have consulted directly with CEOs, authors, celebrities, and entrepreneurs as well as experts in varied fields such as digital marketing, finance, relationships, spirituality, health, business, beauty, and theology to produce content, products, events, websites, and marketing strategies that take their businesses to the next level.

I am the bestselling author of *Ratchet Mom: The Working Mothers Secret to Balancing Career and Family Without Selling Yourself Short*. My articles have been published in InterVarsity's Student Leadership Journal and in Asbury's Seedbed Publication where I co-authored the book *Motherhood as a Spiritual Practice*. I am a GetPulsed Fitness instructor. I love to watch movies with popcorn and I play the flute and piano (but not at the same time). Originally from Tennessee, I now live in Atlanta, GA with my family of six super-active, almost teenage ninja turtles.

In the end, all I really want is for women to find a place of courage that leads us to make the decisions needed to protect ourselves and our children. You've already taken responsibility for where you are in life, but now you must decide what you're going to do. Determine how you're going to move to a higher place and simply do it. Remember, doing nothing is also a decision. It's the decision to give away your personal power and allow someone else to think for you. That should not be an option for you.

About the Author

CARITA MONTGOMERY is a prayer coach, leading hospitality sales professional, as well as life coach, whose global platform has reached and served thousands of people. From a wife and mother of three to a successful corporate executive and entrepreneur, Carita's courage and determination has inspired people worldwide and helped countless audiences break through to discover what is already on the inside of them.

Carita is the Founder and Chief Executive of Uknowtoo.com, one of the country's premiere training companies with emphasis on personal and business development training. Carita has created workshops and programs that have transformed the lives of men and women and companies throughout the country.

A noted prayer coach and inspirational leader of the Everything Prayer Call and Annual Conference, she has touched the lives of thousands through prayer and meditation. Carita has dedicated years to restoring confidence through prayer.

The prestigious awards and honors bestowed upon Carita for her extensive work in hospitality sales include JHM Rookie of the Year award (six months with the company),

Marriott's Chairman's Circle Award, Residence Inn by Marriott Director of Sales of the Year (two consecutive years), JHM Sales Culture Leader of the Year Award and more.

Carita and her family lives, plays, and works in the metro Atlanta area. She is on stages around the world, working alongside her world-class team, committed to motivating the masses.

www.ingramcontent.com/pod-product-compliance
Lightning Source LLC
LaVergne TN
LVHW051157080426
835508LV00021B/2678